Tech-Free Activities When It Rains

by
Rebecca Phillips-Bartlett

Minneapolis, Minnesota

Credits
All images are courtesy of Shutterstock.com, unless otherwise specified. With thanks to Getty Images, Thinkstock Photo, iStockphoto, and Adobe Stock.

Recurring images – Natalia Toropova, A Aleksii, Tartila, Anna Frajtova, nataka, GoodStudio, Perfect_kebab, EllenM, ssinopti, Voin_Sveta, WARNING aommaneesri. Cover – Illonajalll Aksenova Natalya, Aleksandar Dickov, Anna Kucherova, chaythawin, Daboost, Nik Merkulov, chaythawin, AlexFilim, xpixel, Vadym Zaitsev, yusufdemirci, Apolinarias, Bunwit Unseree, Leona Milori, halimqd, Pikovit, sinoptic. 4–5 – art of line, IrinaK, rangizzz, Smit, onsuda. 6–7 – Cast Of Thousands, Evgenyrychko, Queenmoonlite Studio, Illonajalll. 8–9 – PeopleImages.com, tmicons, bangchuck, Pogorelova Olga, MaryDesy. 10–11 – Andrei Armiagov, KawaiiS, KAWEESTUDIO, Mikhail Turov, Nataliia K, studio BM, valkoinen, vitaliy. 12–13 – ajt, Aleksandar Dickov, Eric Isselee, Gallinago_media, hsagencia, natthawut ngoensanthia, Pixel-Shot. 14–15 – alinabuphoto, Bryony van der Merwe, jwu, New Africa, Sergey Sklezhev, Vanatchanan. 16–17 – Alexlukin, FamVeld, Gary Saxe, Oleg Kopyov, Khorzhevska, Tapat.p, xpixel, Peopleimages. 18–19 – Ann in the uk, d1skk, FotoHelin, M. Unal Ozmen, prisma, VitaminCo, Karen Roach. 20–21 – AlenKadr, Anton-Burakov, BartTa, Monkey Business Images, La fotisto, Moskvich19771977. 22–23 – FamVeld, Manoonson Sonon, Roman Samokhin, xpixel, SolStock.

Bearport Publishing Company Product Development Team
Publisher: Jen Jenson; Director of Product Development: Spencer Brinker; Managing Editor: Allison Juda; Editor: Cole Nelson; Associate Editor: Naomi Reich; Associate Editor: Tiana Tran; Art Director: Colin O'Dea; Designer: Kim Jones; Designer: Kayla Eggert; Product Development Specialist: Owen Hamlin

Library of Congress Cataloging-in-Publication Data

Names: Phillips-Bartlett, Rebecca, 1999- author.
Title: Tech-free activities when it rains / by Rebecca Phillips-Bartlett.
Description: Minneapolis, Minnesota : Bearport Publishing Company, [2025] | Series: Unplugging | Includes index.
Identifiers: LCCN 2024036746 (print) | LCCN 2024036747 (ebook) | ISBN 9798892327466 (library binding) | ISBN 9798892327961 (paperback) | ISBN 9798892328333 (ebook)
Subjects: LCSH: Amusements--Juvenile literature. | Outdoor recreation--Juvenile literature. | Rain and rainfall--Miscellenea--Juvenile literature.
Classification: LCC GV1203 .P483 2025 (print) | LCC GV1203 (ebook) | DDC 790--dc23/eng/20240903
LC record available at https://lccn.loc.gov/2024036746
LC ebook record available at https://lccn.loc.gov/2024036747

© 2025 BookLife Publishing
This edition is published by arrangement with BookLife Publishing.

North American adaptations © 2025 Bearport Publishing Company. All rights reserved. No part of this publication may be reproduced in whole or in part, stored in any retrieval system, or transmitted in any form or by any means, electronic, mechanical, photocopying, recording, or otherwise, without written permission from the publisher.

For more information, write to Bearport Publishing, 5357 Penn Avenue South, Minneapolis, MN 55419.

Contents

Unplugging. 4
When It Rains 6
Rules of the Rain 8
Dress for the Rain. 10
Look for Animals 12
Start an Unplugging Diary 14
Create a Dam 16
Make a Rain Gauge 18
Build a Waterproof Den 20
Paint with Mud. 22
Plan Your Day. 23
Glossary 24
Index. 24

Unplugging

Devices can be fun, but there is a whole world to **explore** outside. Unplugging is all about turning off screens and having some tech-free fun!

When It Rains

Not all rainy days have to be spent indoors. If you use a little bit of **imagination**, there is no end to the fun you can have when it rains.

What will you need to get started?

This book

A grown-up

Your imagination

A rainy day

7

Rules of the Rain

There are a few rules we should always follow to stay safe while we have fun in the rain. Read these rules, and ask a grown-up if you have any questions.

- TRY NOT TO SPLASH OTHERS AROUND YOU.

- STAY WITH AN ADULT AT ALL TIMES.

- DRESS FOR THE WEATHER.

- DO NOT PLAY NEAR OR ON THE ROAD. DRIVERS MAY HAVE A HARD TIME SEEING YOU BECAUSE OF THE RAIN.

- HEAD INSIDE IF YOU HEAR THUNDER OR SEE LIGHTNING.

Dress for the Rain

Playing in the rain can be fun, but sometimes it can be chilly. It is important to keep safe and dress warm for rainy weather.

Sweater

Boots

Umbrella

Hat

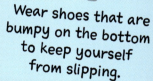

Wear shoes that are bumpy on the bottom to keep yourself from slipping.

Socks

Raincoat

Gloves

Waterproof pants

After your rainy adventure, make sure to change into warm, dry clothes. This will keep you from catching a cold.

11

Look for Animals

When it rains, some animals try to find places to stay dry. Others come out to enjoy the wet weather. How many animals can you spot?

Snail

Slug

Dog

Duck

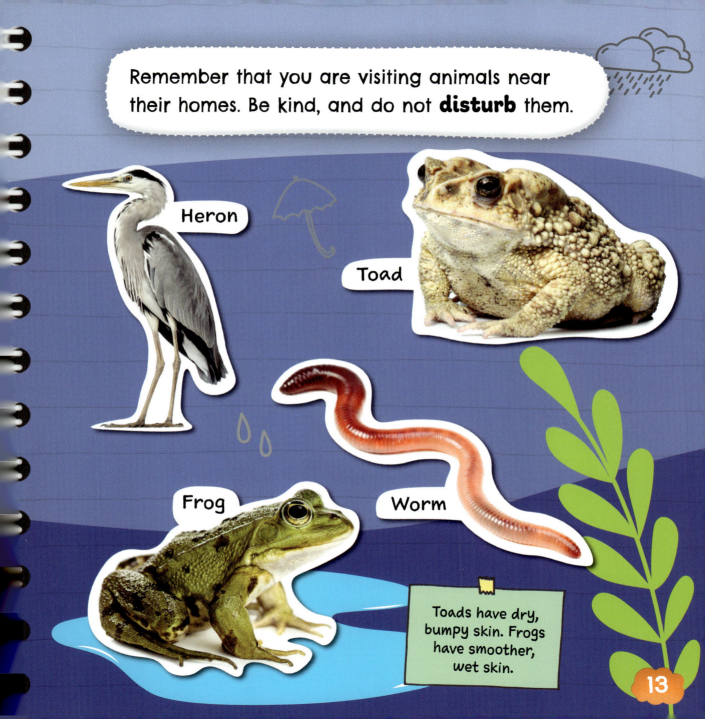

Start an Unplugging Diary

Even on rainy days, there are still ways to connect with nature. Start an unplugging diary at home! Use it to help remember your favorite outdoor adventures.

What you'll need:

A notebook

Pens, pencils, or crayons

Art supplies and decorations

14

STEPS

1. Decorate the front cover of the notebook. Write your name and the following title: *Unplugging Diary*.

2. Think of an outdoor activity you have done.

3. Draw a picture or write about what you did and the things you saw.

> **Tip ★ Tip ★ Tip**
> Use your unplugging diary to remind yourself about the fun things you can do in the rain!

Create a Dam

Dams are walls that hold back water. Beavers create them to keep their watery homes safe. Try building your own dam!

A dam

What you'll need:

A large puddle or small stream

Sticks and stones

STEPS

1. Find a small body of water.

2. Build a wall across the water using sticks and stones.

3. Keep building until your wall blocks the water from coming through.

Could you build a dam to stop paper boats from crossing a puddle?

Make a Rain Gauge

Some days are rainier than others. Make a rain gauge to measure how much rain falls on a wet day. Use an **upcycled** jar to help the planet.

What you'll need:

A jar

A ruler

A marker

*Tip *Tip *Tip*
Make sure the bottom of your jar is flat. This helps you get exact measurements.

STEPS

1. Place the ruler vertically against the jar.

2. Starting from the bottom, mark inches and half-inches along the jar with a marker.

3. Keep marking until you reach the top of the jar.

4. Leave the jar out in the rain. Check how much rain it collects in one hour.

Build a Waterproof Den

Different kinds of animals make different homes. Some build **dens** for themselves and their babies. Try making your own waterproof den!

What you'll need:

Sticks

A waterproof covering

STEPS

1. Lean sticks against one another or prop them against a tree.

2. With a grown-up, add your waterproof covering on top of the den.

3. Go inside and test your den. Do you see or feel any falling water?

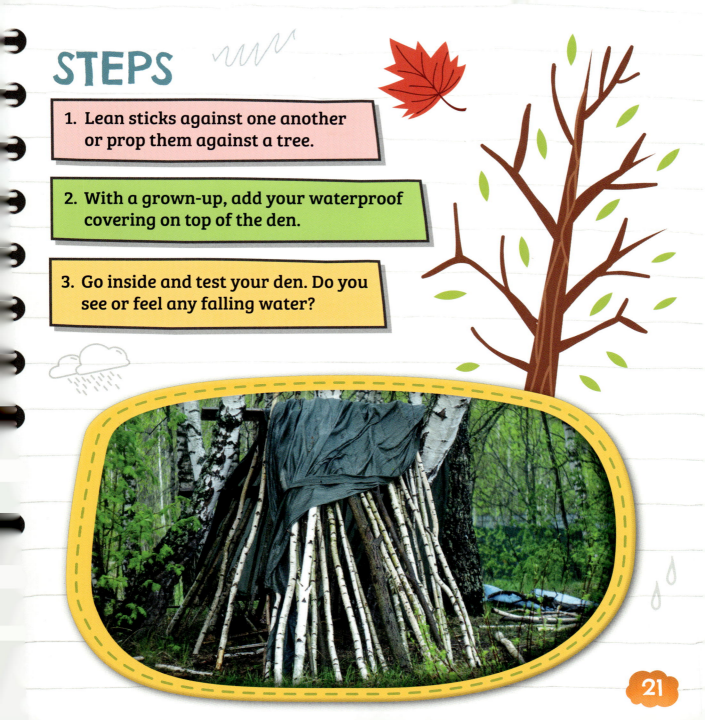

Paint with Mud

Rain can make lots of mud! Use your imagination to make different kinds of art with mud. What will you paint?

What you'll need:

Paper

Mud

*Tip*Tip*Tip*
If the mud is too dry, hold it up to the rain to get it wet.

Plan Your Day

Now that you know what to do, put your screens away. Get outside and play in the rain for some tech-free fun! What will you do first?

Glossary

dams walls or barriers built to hold back water

dens hidden places where animals sleep

devices machines such as tablets or smartphones

disturb to bother someone or something

explore to search in order to discover something

imagination the ability to have many ideas and think creatively

upcycled something old turned into something new

waterproof able to keep water from passing through

Index

animals 5, 12–13, 20
dens 20–21
diary 14–15
grown-ups 7–8, 21
mud 22
puddles 16–17
sticks 16–17, 20–21
stones 16–17
unplugging 4–5, 14–15
waterproof 11, 20–21